SYSTEMS

Using Contrarian Thinking to Power Your Career or Business Engine

COACH TEDDY EDOUARD

COACHING FOR BETTER LEARNING

Print ISBN: 978-1-7377608-9-4

CONTENTS

Who should read this book?

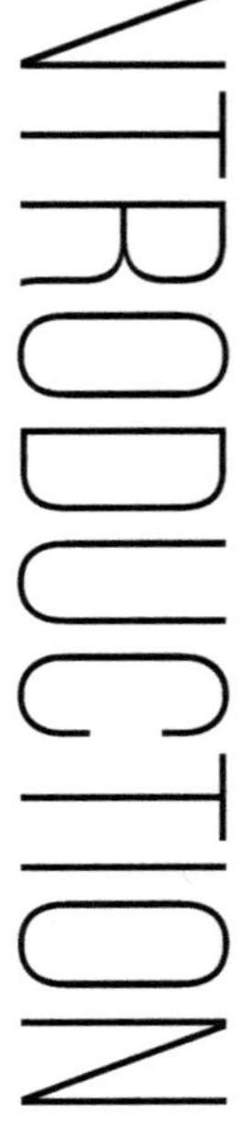

The essence of the independent mind lies not in what it thinks, but in how it thinks.

— LARRY OSBORNE

This book aims to introduce professionals who want to think for themselves to contrarian thinking. It offers them a set of guidelines or a *system* to shape their own thought processes.

Specifically, it is designed for those who don't want to waste their time fitting in, going with the flow or following the status quo—practices that usually lead nowhere.

This practical book focuses on the applied uses of contrarian thinking. It's not for you if you want to philosophize about contrarian thinking or debate it. It is a simple and concise publication intended as a practical tool for professionals, entrepreneurs and students who want to develop and sharpen their thinking to more effectively power their career decisions and endeavors. In other words, it is about using thoughts and ideas to rise above the noise of the marketplace. It will show you how to think and stand for something different.

Coaching for Better Learning (CBL) has prepared this book for people who believe that if they think for themselves, they can grab the wheel of their lives, shape their careers, and work towards goals that they want to accomplish instead of doing what they are told.

If you…

> - are tired of fitting in and maintaining the status quo
> - want to direct your life instead of following others
> - desire to lead instead of hiding behind titles and excuses
> - want to think on your feet and own your thoughts
> - are comfortable with being different
> - want to avoid being a victim of society's biases
> - do not crave popularity or attention
> - want to sound informed and educated
> - want to get past superficial information
> - desire to develop critical thinking skills
> - want to get paid to think critically

…then, you need to keep reading.

Our Promise

We know your time is valuable, so we designed this book so you can read it in one or two sittings. You can also opt to read only the chapters that meet your immediate needs or goals. In other words, we get right to the point.

However, we also provide additional resources on contrarian thinking for those who desire to dig deeper. Once you understand the basics, you can work on your thinking system and game plan at your leisure.

This book focuses on foundational knowledge about contrarian thinking, offering concrete strategies to help professionals and entrepreneurs work on building a contrarian thinker mindset and system. You won't just find theory and feel-good maxims. We give you an effective framework to help you get going today. You'll receive enough information and resources to decide whether cultivating a contrarian way of life is right for you and how to get started if it is.

Chapter 1	defines contrarian thinking and its origin.
Chapter 2	presents key principles of contrarian thinking.
Chapter 3	discusses why contrarian thinking is important for professionals and entrepreneurs.

Chapter 4	provides concrete examples of contrarian thinking in the business world.
Chapter 5	presents thought leaders in contrarian thinking.
Chapter 6	shares strategies for developing contrarian thinking.
Chapter 7	discusses how contrarian thinking impacts one's personal, professional and business life.
Chapter 8	provides resources for future contrarian thinkers.

If you're ready to start a new way of thinking and a new life, let's get started!

What Is Contrarian Thinking and What Is Its Origin?

Contrarian thinking, at its best, simply asks, "Is this really true?" It speaks up when the politically correct answer or the conventional wisdom doesn't match reality - when things simply don't work the way everyone says they should.

— CHRISTOPHER HITCHENS

Contrarian thinking is a concept that, at first glance, may actually seem annoying. At its core, it's simply thinking differently from the majority. It means questioning popular beliefs instead of accepting everything the way you see it. It may seem simple, but it's a powerful tool that can lead to extraordinary results when the majority fails due to their insistence on using outdated strategies and thinking.

In a sense, contrarian thinking is the way of thinking that many of the world's most visionary figures used to achieve their goals and make the world a better place. After all, what makes them visionary is the fact that they brought different thoughts and ideas to the world.

Let's get into the details of how this works.

The Origins of Contrarian Thinking

Contrarian thinking has most likely been around since the earliest days of humanity. After all, it's the driver behind most of our species' sociological and technological advancements. When most cave dwellers were hunting with their bare hands, some contrarian thinker eventually picked up a stick and sharpened it into a spear, changing the world forever.

In fact, there are plenty of examples of contrarian thinkers in recorded history. Leonardo da Vinci was one. He took contrarian stances against the scientific community with almost all of his inventions. Even his art went against the mainstream trends of his era. Yet, we're still talking about him five hundred years later.

Steve Jobs is a more recent example. Jobs saw the way technology was being developed, realized that it was aimed primarily at tech-savvy users, and found ways to streamline the most popular technologies for a wider audience. His innovation led to one of the most successful companies in the world: Apple.

Modern history is full of examples of contrarian thinking: George Washington Carver, Elon Musk, Harriet Tubman, Jeff Bezos, Martin Luther King Jr., Richard Branson and Frederick Douglass. They all stood their ground against popular beliefs, convergent thinking and the status quo.

Let's get more concrete about contrarian thinking.

As we said earlier, contrarians embrace unpopular beliefs, ideas and thoughts. However, they don't just do this to be difficult or stand out. To be productive, they must have a purpose. So, what is that purpose?

Well, it typically happens with issues where the crowd is doing something poorly, and the contrarian wants to try another approach.

To give you an exaggerated example, imagine if most businesses are using an extremely wasteful business model. Imagine they are spending millions of dollars trying to have employees use their personal cars to deliver entire warehouses worth of products across the country.

No one does that, of course, but a contrarian would see just how wasteful the companies were and decide to do something different. Perhaps they'd devise a plan to consolidate distribution efforts by hiring tractor-trailer drivers to carry large loads to multiple locations.

That's what contrarian thinkers do. They take a different approach from the ineffective masses to reach a more desirable result.

Contrarian thinking can be found in practically every group, but it's most common and impactful in politics and businesses.

In a political sense, people who stand out from the crowd and take new approaches tend to be the ones that go down in history for positive reasons. They are the people who devise laws and policies that lead to real change with widespread impact.

Additionally, you see contrarian thinkers in the business world all the time. Investors who make massive returns on investments (ROIs) typically don't go along with their peers; companies that end up skyrocketing to the top of their industry usually do something different than those that came before them. It's the innovators who come up with the next big thing, and innovation doesn't come from copying everyone else.

Start contrarian thinking today.

Because contrarian thinkers are usually the ones who see the best results, it may be in your best interest to start thinking like one today. We have several resources available to help you out. Keep reading to unlock the secrets to your success.

Key Principles in Contrarian Thinking

The best opportunities are often ones where you're being contrarian. That doesn't mean being contrarian for contrarian's sake, but it means you're thoughtful about the risks of following the crowd.

—DAVID SZE

Contrarian thinking seems simple at first. At its core, it seems to go directly against the grain and established ways of solving problems.

However, it's more complicated than just saying "no" when everyone says "yes" or vice-versa. Every successful contrarian has guided their contradictory ideas and methods with basic principles.

While you go through your contrarian development, we want to make sure you go about it the right way and find the success you want. That's why we've compiled a list of the key principles of contrarian thinking to guide your development. These principles worked for countless contrarian leaders throughout history.

It's not just about disagreeing.

Contrarian thinking isn't simply disagreeing with whatever everyone else says. (That's just being obnoxious.) They don't argue that the sky is yellow because everyone says it's blue. No, a contrarian takes the opposite stance when it counts and when there's a real benefit in doing so. It is much more about an individualistic thought process than being difficult or saying the opposite of what everyone else says to get attention, like the annoying kid in school.

It's key to understand this distinction so you don't fall down the proverbial rabbit hole of disagreeing with everyone.

Contrarians notice when the masses are all following the same paradigm for their business, sociological or political endeavors, and the results simply aren't what they could be. For example, they look at people investing in a hot new stock all at once, determine that the stock will become overvalued, and then start buying up less popular stocks that show long-term stability instead.

A contrarian sees where people are making mistakes, and they take the opposite route to achieve different, more desirable results.

Start from scratch.

Contrarians also don't simply disagree with the masses. Very little of a contrarian's effort is spent actually arguing with others. Instead, they put that effort towards looking at the problem in question with a clean slate. Then, they will seek out as much impartial information as possible, refusing to allow popular opinion or preconceived notions to persuade them when the facts are saying something else.

Resist pressure.

People don't like to be challenged. Due to the nature of contrarian thinking in business and the job market, many contrarians face a lot of pressure to conform or accept the opinions of the masses.

Good contrarians, the ones who make a difference, are the ones who can resist this peer pressure and blaze their own trails. They're individuals with strong backbones, and none of them are easily persuaded.

Take calculated risks.

One thing all contrarians have in common is that they're willing to take risks. After all, there's a reason the masses all go one way: it's usually the safest way, or at least they think it is.

By simply being a contrarian, one embraces a more risk-filled lifestyle. And yes, it's a business model that could sometimes end up blowing up in your face.

However, we're not telling you to run off and take nonsensical risks. Remember: it's not about disagreeing for the sake of being different; it's about finding what works better.

The types of risks contrarians take are calculated. For example, let's say you had $400 of Dogecoin at the beginning of the big crypto-buying binge, and you noticed the masses suddenly buying it up. This would have caused your measly $400 investment to grow exponentially. If you were like everyone else, you'd have kept buying more, hoping the value of your Dogecoin would stay strong. As history now shows, many people lost money because of that mindset.

A contrarian would have seen their Dogecoin growing in value rapidly, realized that it was due to crash soon, and started selling before the bubble hit its peak.

While it's true that people who sold a little too early risked missing out on even larger profits, they acknowledged the flaws of the masses and got out before all their profits disappeared.

Embrace rational thought.

Above all else, a contrarian takes a rational approach to problem solving and philosophy. This is what sets them apart from the crowd.

Most people are typically driven by emotional factors that cloud their judgment. Remaining stoic in your pursuit of rational thought processes and solutions is the most vital part of being a contrarian thinker.

Always focus on education and learning.

When we say to always focus on education, we don't mean constantly seeking out new degrees and spending a lot of your would-be business capital on tuition. We mean to keep learning new things.

Every aspect of contrarianism requires you to be highly knowledgeable and informed about the topics you take a stance on. That is why you need a *system* to keep yourself educated and informed.

If you're an entrepreneur, you need to constantly stay up-to-date with the current trends in your industry, how other businesses are performing, and what your competitors are doing. After all, you can't take the opposite route if you have no idea what the crowd is doing in the first place.

If you're just trying to use contrarian thinking to better your personal life, take a look at how other people around you are leading theirs. If you want better results, you have to know what they're going through and their stances on hot topics.

For your professional life, you have to put in the time and effort to understand your employer's business processes, where they fall short, and how you can really provide value to the company. It takes time and effort to do all this. But if you're not taking the time to do those things, you'll be stuck in your position like everyone else.

Whatever you're using contrarianism for, make educating yourself a top priority.

Learn from the best.

Being a contrarian also doesn't mean that you reject the opinions and experiences of everyone else on the planet. Rather, contrarian thinkers learn from selected experts in various fields.

Many experts have implemented innovative ideas into their lives, investments and businesses far better than you have. Taking the time to learn from those individuals and benefit from their experiences can help you on your journey.

This means following high-profile contrarians on social media, networking with contrarians of all experience levels at events and on social media platforms like LinkedIn and Twitter, attending seminars and taking advantage of any other learning opportunities that you come across.

However, be careful that you don't end up following another set of masses. Don't go from following the mainstream crowd to following another on the opposite end of the spectrum.

Famous contrarian investors, contrarian thinking groups and the people you meet while networking are great to learn from. Still, the whole point of being a contrarian is that you think for yourself.

Use positive contrarian thinking.

Contrarianism is just like anything else. When used appropriately and with the right intentions, it can be an amazing tool that changes your life and the lives of those around you. However, being overzealous about it can have the opposite effect.

When you use contrarian thinking, make sure you're doing it with good intentions, and always make sure that it has some sort of potential positive outcome. Your efforts should be well-researched, rational, and of course, beneficial to those around you. Don't tear things down just for the sake of being different.

Follow these principles and master contrarianism.

Contrarian thinking relies on the principles discussed in this chapter to lead one to success. If you want to develop a contrarian mindset effectively, you'll have to keep these in your mind and *learning system* as you do so.

Why Is Contrarian Thinking Important for Professionals and Entrepreneurs?

CHAPTER III

The only way to consistently stay ahead of the game is to adopt a long-term view and, if appropriate, with a strong contrarian spin.

— MARK MOBIUS

Contrarian thinking, or the act of taking the opposite stance of the majority, has been a key part of innovation since the earliest years of civilization. One cannot innovate by following the crowd. It's simple.

From Leonardo da Vinci to Martin Luther King Jr., countless historical figures were contrarians who dared to go off the beaten path to find exceptional results. In many cases, these contrarians have had a tremendous impact on the modern world. They've innovated our technology, changed our laws and policies for the better, and created business models that facilitate seamless global trade.

The contrarian viewpoint is crucial for professionals and entrepreneurs, but why is that? What is it about contrarian thinking that has led to such a long history of individual success and widespread positive impact?

Let's look at the details.

1. Contrarian thinking increases personal success.

Personal success is a driving factor in most people's lives. We certainly won't challenge that idea. The good thing about contrarian thinking is that it often increases personal success AND has widespread effects on entire companies, communities and even the world.

This is because it encourages new approaches. Often, most of an industry or population will settle on a system that works, find some success, and then stick with it without ever attempting anything new. They're playing it safe and going with what works.

That approach leads to stagnation, and it ensures that less effective parts of the system are never worked on or improved. Eventually, this type of behavior ruins companies or causes them to miss out on major opportunities.

As Elon Musk said, "Some people don't like change, but you need to embrace change if the alternative is a disaster."

The contrarian viewpoint avoids those problems because it separates itself from the status quo. It acknowledges the current system's shortcomings, and it actively looks for a new way to do things, even when everyone else is hesitant to try.

As a result, contrarians often find new, better ways to accomplish their goals. Although there's some risk involved, they often see massive returns on their investments as a result.

2. Contrarian thinking aids larger groups.

Contrarian thinking isn't just important to individuals. It has aided society since the beginning of humanity's history and revolutionized the way we do things.

After all, where would we be if Johannes Gutenberg did not revolutionize book production with the printing press? Or if a group of forward-thinking scientists did not develop the Advanced Research Projects Agency Network (ARPANET), the foundation of the internet?

Even Einstein's work, which has shaped nearly every scientific field for almost a century, was contrarian. Today he's revered as one of the greatest minds of all time, but that certainly wasn't always the case. The scientific community fought hard against his theory of relativity in favor of the traditional view of physics. His work led to the development of quantum physics, which is today driving some of the most advanced high-tech research around.

3. *It shapes lives and changes societies.*

As you can see, contrarian thinking is more than just somebody being complicated or an oddball. It's the driving force behind billionaires leading the lives they do, and it's the reason society has developed as much as it has.

Without contrarians pushing innovation, the world would likely be far behind where it is today; while the status quo is reliable, it's simply not innovative.

Embracing contrarian thinking is an effective way to grow personally, improve your career or businesses endeavors, and positively impact society. Driving innovation and promoting progress in any field require that professionals distance themselves and their thinking from popular thinking and limitations. In the next chapter, we'll look at some examples of this.

Concrete Examples of Contrarian Thinking in the Business World

The overwhelming majority of people are comfortable with consensus, but successful investors tend to have a contrarian bent.

— SETH KLARMAN

By now, you know all about what contrarian thinking is, why it's important, and how it can help you succeed. We don't think that's enough, though.

People don't really understand an idea until they're presented with concrete examples of the idea in the real world and how it impacts those involved. So, we've created a list of several examples of contrarian thinking in the business world to drive the message home.

Let's get started.

The Early Days of Facebook

Mark Zuckerberg didn't invent the concept of social media. We all remember how popular Myspace was while Zuckerberg was still in college, and AOL was blazing a trail with its chatrooms as early as the 1990s. However, Zuckerberg did revolutionize social media and turned it into the global powerhouse it is today.

How'd he do it? Well, he saw the flaws in the previous social media models. They were clunky, non-conducive for businesses, and generally offered a poor experience. So, he took a different route.

Zuckerberg started experimenting on his college campus to work out the kinks of his new social media model. He devised easier ways for people to find each other and better ways to disperse content to large audiences. He completely reworked how communication was executed by taking different approaches than Myspace and other online options of the period.

As a result, Facebook is now one of the largest companies on earth, has an influence on consumer decisions around the globe, and is a key part of not only everyday interactions and relationships, but of brand-building and business growth.

Viking Kitchen Appliances

As a powerhouse of the kitchen appliance world, Viking is a name that experienced chefs have come to respect around the globe. However, it wasn't always seen as such an amazing product provider. When the company's founder was getting started, every manufacturer he approached thought he was working on a pipe dream.

Fred Carl Jr., the founder of Viking, started out trying to make an at-home kitchen range for his wife based on her grandmother's old-fashioned range. He couldn't simply buy appliances because they'd become exclusive to the restaurant sector.

He took the concept of a restaurant-quality range, scaled it down and reworked it to make sense in a home environment.

Once he began building a range for his wife, he wanted to start manufacturing them for the consumer market, and he began approaching manufacturers with his design. Almost all of them turned him down because "home cooks don't want restaurant-style ranges." At least, that's what they thought.

Once Frank found a manufacturer willing to work with him, his new company skyrocketed, and the company now makes some of the most sought-after home ranges on the market. He's received praise from the world's finest chefs, and people are willing to spend large sums on a quality Viking range.

Warren Buffett's Impressive Investment Record

If you've dabbled in investments for even a short time, we're willing to bet you've heard of Warren Buffett and his investment empire. By simply playing the stock market, Warren Buffett has amassed a vast fortune, and he has a substantial following of investors who look to him for guidance.

However, he didn't gain all that success by going with the flow. His investment philosophy is built entirely around taking advantage of the masses' shortsightedness.

Warren Buffett doesn't invest in the same companies at the same time as other major investment firms. He waits until large groups of investors make shortsighted investments and lets those investments go down the drain while he invests in the long-term success of companies that aren't getting as much attention.

As you can see, Warren Buffett's contrarian tactics have brought him quite a bit of success.

His long-term investment strategy in a short-term market can be summed up with one of his best quotes: "Someone is sitting in the shade today because someone planted a tree a long time ago."

Everyday People

Famous people aren't the only concrete examples of contrarianism. There are plenty of ordinary people just like you who live contrarian lifestyles, and you're probably surrounded by them without even knowing it.

Let's get into some of the everyday examples of contrarianism that you're likely to see daily.

The Political Contrarian Friend

We all have at least one friend who seems to disagree with everything related to politics. Whether they go against the mainstream views of whatever party is in office, or they just flat-out reject all political parties and prefer to look at the political landscape from an independent perspective, they're contrarian by nature.

You may notice your friend posting their opinions on social media when they completely contradict the popular opinion. This friend may also be like your coworker who voices their unique opinions during their lunch break.

Sometimes, people like this may be confused with the opposite of whatever your stance is, and that might be the case. However, it's important to note that a contrarian isn't just someone who disagrees with you while following another form of groupthink. A contrarian is someone who looks at the situation from a purely individual approach.

The Everyday Crypto Investor

With the crypto craze kicking into full swing and hitting the mainstream, more and more investors are buying digital currency with the hopes of getting massive ROIs. This has created a system of financial speculation very similar to the stock market. Crowd followers tend to invest in the same volatile coins and inflate their value, just like a hot stock.

However, contrarians are starting to invest in crypto, too. As the most popular coins reach their breaking point, contrarians begin investing in low-value coins that are likely to pick up steam very quickly. They get ahead of the curve, and when the masses jump aboard, they start selling to avoid the huge value drop that usually follows.

The Coworker Making Waves

Let's say you work for a company where everybody does the same thing and more or less receives the same results. However, one employee bucks the trend while getting the job done faster, more effectively and without wasting as much time or energy as everyone else. That person impresses the boss and gives his input from time to time, and the boss takes him seriously.

In all likelihood, that employee is a contrarian. He sees that the standard system doesn't work as well as it could, so he developed his own solutions. As a result, he experiences more success in the workplace than the average, more compliant employee.

Learn from these examples.

From renowned professionals to everyday people, these are all examples from which you can learn. As you continue your journey to contrarian thinking, keep these real-world examples in mind and try to model your approach after them. Remember, it's not just about being different; it's about being different for the right reasons.

Leaders in Contrarian Thinking

When your views are truly contrarian, they are inevitably uncomfortable. Courage and the ability to withstand pain are required.

— MICHAEL STEINHARDT

We are provided with many resources on contrarian thinking in modern times, but sometimes it's best to learn directly from history's greatest examples. After all, they're the ones that went from average joes to business moguls and world-changing figures.

Today, we want to give you an overview of some of the finest contrarians in history.

As a famous Zen Proverb says, "It takes a wise man to learn from his mistakes, but an even wiser man to learn from others."

Let's get started!

Samuel Brannan

Samuel Brannan was a publicist at the beginning of the California Gold Rush. As companies and prospectors realized that there were massive deposits of gold in the state, they fixated on collecting as much gold as possible to make their fortune.

Samuel Brannan decided to take a different route. Instead of chasing the gold itself, he bought every shovel he could find in San Francisco. Then, he took to the streets and let everyone else know about the impending gold rush.

Naturally, the masses leaped at the idea of finding a fortune lodged into the ground. People came from all across the country to fight over the gold harvest. Not Samuel Brannan, though. He didn't care about finding gold. He only sold the supplies the gold seekers needed, and his foresight and planning made him one of the only sources in the area.

When asked about the move, Brannan said, "The real money's in the shovels. Not the gold."

Henry Ford

Henry Ford is the main reason we drive cars today. He didn't invent the combustion engine, and he didn't even make the first motorized vehicle. What he did develop were the mass manufacturing techniques that brought cars to the masses.

Henry faced skepticism every step of the way. Society at the time was built on the backs of horses, which had been used for thousands of years, so no one saw the need to switch over to these newfangled automobiles. But, of course, the switch changed society forever.

This move also led to the consumer market we have today. Henry paid more than any other manufacturer, nearly doubling his employees' wages so they would have enough money to afford the products they were making. In other words, he created the products and the market to buy those products. This mass consumer market still drives many of the world's economies.

Martin Luther King Jr.

Dr. King needs no introduction. As a civil rights leader, he led a non-violent movement that shook the structure of the US discrimination machine to its core. The notion that social change could be accomplished through demonstration, through sit-ins, and through shaping of public opinion – rather than just public policy – was a powerful one. Dr. King and his fellow leaders influenced Washington's political leaders. They obliged to take action to pass anti-discrimination laws that impacted the whole nation, changing rules that had been in place for over a century.

George Washington Carver

Despite experiencing the oppression of racism, Carver persevered to become one of the most distinguished black scientists of the 20th century.

After completing high school, he was initially accepted by Highland University in Kansas. However, he was refused entry due to his race. George didn't let this setback deter him. He did odd jobs until he was accepted by another institution, Iowa State University, becoming its first black pupil. There, he attained a degree in agriculture and a master's degree in agricultural science—accomplishments that seemed impossible at that time for blacks.

Carver's work was extensive and earned him national recognition. He went on to teach as the first black professor at Iowa State. He also became famous for his methods of preventing soil depletion and developing organic fertilizers and peanut products. His methods are still used in agricultural practices today.

Frederick Douglass

Slaveholders argued that slaves lacked the intellectual ability to be free American citizens. Frederick Douglass was living proof that their argument was baseless.

Douglass was a slave who learned to read and write by exchanging bread with poor, white boys and tracing letters in his master's son's schoolbooks. Eventually, he escaped slavery after enduring severe physical and psychological abuse. At every turn, he encountered prejudice that made it difficult for him to get work to sustain himself. But he didn't let that stop him.

He was an avid reader, an eloquent speaker and a national leader in the abolitionist movement. He also went on to publish three autobiographies (yes, that's right—three). He understood that his personal story was a powerful tool for change and inspiration. Throughout his life, he remained committed to social justice. He advocated for the rights of all and was active in the woman suffrage movement.

Harriet Tubman

Harriet Tubman was dubbed the "Moses of the people," and for a good reason.

As a child, Harriet was often beaten by slaveowners and was once hit by a two-pound weight. As a result, she got narcolepsy or "sleeping spells," which affected her for the rest of her life. But like other contrarian thinkers, the incident pushed her towards making a better life for herself and others.

Using her ingenuity and courage, Tubman led numerous slaves to freedom through the Underground Railroad, a series of secret routes and safe houses. She conducted these dangerous expeditions personally, risking her life repeatedly.

And she didn't stop there. She served several important roles during the American Civil War and then fought for women's suffrage after the war ended. She also cared for the elderly and raised money to build schools for newly freed people. Indeed, her whole life was marked by resilience, ingenuity and bravery. She once stated, "I never ran my train off the track and I never lost a passenger."

Learn from the best.

These role models in contrarian thinking illustrate both the concept and its effects. Each person faced challenges but succeeded in impacting the world by refusing to follow what everyone else was doing. There are many more examples that you can look up to, and we encourage you to check out our other resources on the subject.

Whatever you do, we hope that you learn to take calculated risks that go against the mainstream method. As Elon Musk said, "Take risks now and do something bold. You won't regret it."

CHAPTER VI

Strategies for Developing Contrarian Thinking

*Try your hardest to combat atrophy and routine.
To question the obvious and the given is an
essential element of the maxim 'de omnibus
dubitandum' [All is to be doubted]*

— CHRISTOPHER HITCHENS

It would be great if you could simply read a short book and suddenly turn your life around with a new way of thinking, but we know it doesn't usually work that way.

Becoming a successful contrarian isn't just a question of reading the definition and deciding to think differently. It requires you to be proactive, put effort into your thought process, establish a system and spend time practicing this way of thinking about and seeing the world.

That can be a bit difficult, and you likely won't see major results immediately. However, we guarantee that, with time, contrarian thinking will lead to breakthroughs you would never have thought possible.

To help you develop your sense of contrarianism effectively, we've created a framework and list of strategies you can adapt to create your contrarian thinking system and approach life situations.

Specifically, in most situations, your contrarian thinking endeavors should follow strategic steps, actions and anything else you judge necessary. Start with the framework below. This framework gives you top-level concepts you should focus on to prepare yourself and your thinking.

FRAMEWORK

- **Status Quo:** Identify the status quo, traditional conventions and current trends.

- **Information:** Collect data, market trends, research, books, websites and publications on your topic or field of interest.

- **Thought Leaders:** Identify leaders and experts on your topic or field of interest.

- **Events:** Find conferences, webinars and seminars on the topic.

- **Context/Culture:** Identify the impact of the topic or field on cultures and the influence of cultures on the subject.

- **The Big Picture:** Understand the whole system or sector and its parts.

> ➤ **Questions:** Ask and research critical questions.

> ➤ **Observations:** Pay close attention to leaders, ideas, headlines, market trends and government regulations.

> ➤ **Intense Reading:** Read intensively on the topic or the field.

> ➤ **Pain point:** Identify the issues that keep employers, companies and leaders awake at night.

The framework is not an exhaustive list, and it presents concrete steps you can follow. However, you should use your best judgment; how you think and act will vary depending on your situation and culture.

Now let's discuss some key strategies.

1: Be greedy when others are fearful.

This strategy stems from Warren Buffett's most famous quote, but it's true. If you see most people starting to hesitate with their stock purchases, or sell their stock outright, take the opposite route.

This strategy is also valid in professional life. For example, would you choose an easy and boring job over one that challenges you to develop your leadership and decision-making skills?

Of course, you should make the best choice for whatever your circumstance happens to be, but over time, you'll see that an independent, contrarian attitude pays off.

2: Think long-term.

A major problem with many professionals is that they tend to think short-term. They jump in and out of love with industries and companies quickly, rarely looking past the following year, quarter or even month.

Have you ever assessed a sector, especially a challenging one, to decide whether to enter and stay in it? Have you ever wondered where your employer will be in five or ten years? How about your current skill set and competencies? Will they still be good enough to bring home the bacon in ten years?

3: Learn about the industry in which you work.

This isn't a direct contrarian action, but it directly affects your ability to use contrarian thinking. After all, you can't make intelligent decisions against popular opinion if you don't understand the industry those popular opinions revolve around. That's why knowledge is such an important part of the framework.

Spend time reading and keeping up to date with every aspect of the industry you invest or work in and look for ways that it's falling behind.

4: Practice separating your views from that of the crowd.

Contrarianism is all about finding fresh perspectives. You can't do that if you remain stuck in your ways and go along with whatever the masses are saying. Practice studying hot topics, discovering the popular opinions and then separating your views from the mainstream to develop them.

With time, these practices will translate into success in your business or professional life.

5: Play devil's advocate.

A good way to develop your contrarian mindset is to play devil's advocate. When discussing polarizing topics, try choosing to stand against the majority every time. Even if you don't technically agree with the stance, taking the other side in a discussion will help you develop your ability to go against the grain.

6: Take the exercise home.

We're all more comfortable at home, and that's the best place to start being a contrarian. When there's a family issue or discussion, don't just side with your closest family members. Practice contrarianism to see the points they don't. Just remain rational and fair while doing it.

If you want to do something to alter your professional mindset, you must also do it in your personal life. It's not only a professional tool; it's an approach to life.

7: Participate in groups.

It's hard to develop a contrarian mindset on your own. After all, you must know the approaches others are taking if you want to look for alternatives.

Meet people with divergent opinions and figure out how a fresh perspective could provide better results. You can do this by joining focus groups and seeking networking opportunities.

8: Get hands-on industry experience.

If you plan on innovating the way a marketing business operates, you should probably have experience with the standard model first. For example, if you're starting a marketing business or working in one, learn how different departments work. Try hiring a marketing company to run your next campaign to see how they operate and explore how they could do better.

9: Focus on being right, not contrarian.

A common mistake for wannabe contrarians is that they object to everything and do the opposite of what everyone else is doing for the sake of being different. A different approach doesn't mean much if it doesn't accomplish anything.

When you start with a fresh perspective, pursue your solution because you've put in the research to know it's right, not just because it's different.

10: Practice resisting pressure.

All contrarians will face loads of peer pressure. The masses typically think they're right, and they'll have no problem telling you you're wrong when you contradict them. (After all, if it were easy to go against the grain, more people would do it.)

Get used to doing things against the crowd and practice resisting peer pressure firmly, professionally and rationally.

11: Reject angry points of view.

Many people who resist popular opinions out of anger think they're contrarians. However, that's not the case.

A contrarian doesn't form their opposing viewpoint because they're mad at the popular opinion. They do so because they have discovered a flaw in that opinion, and they want to find a way to fix it or propose something better. Remember that solid contrarianism is rooted in rationality. You are finding a better way to do things using your mind, not your feelings.

12: Ask tough questions.

It's easy to go with the flow and accept whatever you're told. But to become a contrarian, you'll have to ask tough questions. As Anthony Robbins once said, "Successful people ask better questions. As a result, they get better answers."

13: Make challenging statements.

As a contrarian, you stand against the crowd. Don't do it in silence because that will never make you stand out. Make firm, challenging statements that force the other party to think. However, don't be threatening. Assert yourself so that you can make a difference and accomplish your goals.

14: Listen carefully.

It's easy to get a little big-headed once contrarian thinking has brought you a bit of success. After all, it may seem that you're smarter than everyone else! However, letting it get to your head is a surefire way to stop developing. Always listen to popular opinions and know what's going on while continuing to practice the contrarian way of problem-solving.

15: Stay positive.

Contrarianism is difficult. If you allow yourself to start thinking negatively, you can begin taking contrarian stances out of irritation, and become an annoyance to those closest to you. Again, true contrarianism is rooted in the mind, not the heart. It's about being rational instead of emotional.

Keep a smile on your face, and always try to remain positive.

16: Read a lot.

Reading about a topic is one of the best ways to help yourself grasp the concept. There are a lot of books and blogs dedicated to contrarian thinking, with many of the most notable contrarian minds being behind these resources.

Reading these resources will allow you to peer into the thoughts of successful contrarians and learn about various strategies they have used. Overall, you'll be able to expand your mind with more contrarian information.

In Chapter 8, we've included references to guide you towards top-tier reading material, and we recommend you start with these recommendations to get the most out of your time.

17: Follow contrarians on social media.

Social media is an invaluable tool. Most people just don't use it properly. Instead of following the trendiest influencers or looking at memes all day, try searching for leading contrarians in various fields and follow their social media accounts.

Doing this gives you a brief glimpse into the day-to-day life of contrarian professionals, politicians and entrepreneurs, and you'll pick up tons of priceless information you can use in your own life.

We recommend Peter Thiel, Naval Ravikant, Elon Musk, Nassim Taleb, Warren Buffett and Ursula Burns. These and other high-profile contrarians are likely to share their opinions and secrets to success fairly frequently.

However, don't be afraid to look at contrarians in different industries or lifestyles. Not all of the content will be directly relevant to your interests, but you'll still learn about contrarianism.

18: Join LinkedIn.

LinkedIn is basically a social media platform for professionals, and it's accessible to people of all skill levels.

Take the time to flesh out a profile fully, and then look for contrarian professionals with whom you can interact. You'll find that the majority of business leaders and high-profile investors are on the platform, as well as a lot of people at the same stage of growth and development as you.

The platform allows you to learn from more experienced contrarians and build relationships with other budding contrarians and professional leaders. The relationships you build can pay off with information, guidance, and of course, fellowship.

19: Write op-eds or create opinion videos.

If you have some writing skills or the ability to make videos on social media, a great way to practice contrarianism is to share your opinions with the world. Find a topic you're passionate about, focus on ways to take a contrarian stance, and then present that stance to the masses.

You'll get a bit of flak for it (contrarians always do), but you'll also see contrarianism at work first-hand, and you'll likely persuade a few skeptics to agree with you.

Presenting your stance also has the added benefit of helping you hone and develop your skills. As you make more content, you'll learn how to present your contrarian views more effectively, and you'll be forced to focus on developing meaningful stances rather than just standing against the crowd for the sake of it.

20: Build the right circle.

We learn from those around us and adopt their habits. That's just human nature. So, if you surround yourself with people who follow the crowd, it's no surprise that you'll most likely keep following the crowd yourself.

Instead, seek out friends and peers who are also contrarian. You'll likely have different views from one another, but that allows you to debate from different viewpoints, learn new things and find solutions that you won't get from crowd followers.

Forming the right circle doesn't mean you need to disown your family, drop all your friends and only surround yourself with contrarians. However, it does mean that when you start adding people to your circle, be strategic about it and add those that will help you grow.

21: Constantly focus on development.

Finally, and most importantly, become a lifelong learner, an observer and a seeker of knowledge. Bear in mind that there will always be something new to learn. Contrarianism is all about reconsidering what people know; staying informed and growing is the best way to think independently.

In other words, learning is the best way to stay sharp and alive. As Albert Einstein said, "Once you stop learning, you start dying."

Contrarian Thinking in Your Personal, Professional and Business Life

CHAPTER VII

To succeed as a contrarian, you must recognize what the crowd believes, have concrete justification for why the majority is wrong, and have the patience and conviction to stick with what is, by definition, an unpopular bet.

— **WHITNEY TILSON**

If you read a lot of articles or Google contrarian thinking, you'll find a lot of content regarding contrarian investing. This is due to the world's fixation on financial success. The truth is, while a lot of leading contrarians have become known for their financial acumen (we've mentioned a few), contrarian thinking affects much more than investments.

Contrarian thinking can affect every aspect of life. When used properly and with a specific purpose, contrarianism can make you stand out in the workforce, the job market and even your personal life.

Let's take a look at the details.

How Contrarian Thinking Can Help Your Personal Life

Someone who constantly has an opposing view from their friends, family and peers is often seen as annoying. On the surface, it doesn't seem like a great way to make friends.

However, purposeful contrarianism can actually be beneficial for your relationships.

Purposeful contrarians can often find more beneficial solutions to common problems, and hence, they become an asset to their friends and family. In a sense, you can think of contrarians as wise men and women. Because they're approaching situations rationally and independently, they often figure out problems and provide solutions when others are fixated on emotional solutions.

Being like this helps you stand out as someone people can approach for answers or someone from whom they can expect rational behavior instead of blowups and personal attacks that many have come to expect from others.

There are a lot of examples of contrarian thinking that you can use in your personal life to achieve these results. We'll go over some of the most impactful ones.

Perhaps you've come from a family that can't manage its money well, and your family experienced a lot of financial problems as you were growing up. A contrarian would notice that problem, acknowledge the things their family did that caused financial issues, and then set out to try a different approach.

Rather than living paycheck-to-paycheck while eating out frequently and paying high prices for cable service, a contrarian would learn to make cost-effective meals at home, and opt for one or two affordable streaming services to save big bucks on their monthly expenses.

Maybe you grew up in an area where education and self-improvement weren't the focus of most people. Maybe you've seen a lot of your friends, family members and old schoolmates settle into lackluster lives tainted by lack of opportunities. A contrarian would notice that the lack of dedication to self-education and improvement contributed to those problems. They'd seek out reading material, guidance services and structured hobbies that could set them on the path to a brighter future.

Even your dating game can be dramatically uplifted thanks to contrarian thinking. Think back to your high school and college days when your peers rushed into relationships with people they didn't know, or when they didn't have the emotional ability to commit to such relationships. Those relationships probably ended very quickly and brought very little happiness to the lives of everyone involved.

A contrarian would see that the "date everyone in sight and bounce from relationship to relationship" approach simply wasn't effective. They'd take a more cautious, slow and steady approach to dating, and they'd seek out people with personality traits and lifestyles that complemented their own.

Contrarian thinking can be the difference between a positive personal life filled with happiness and a life that often feels like a chore.

In short, using contrarian thinking, along with the framework and strategies discussed above, might influence the following:

- ➤ How you spend and invest your money
- ➤ What you study
- ➤ Your choice of reading materials
- ➤ How you spend your time and energy
- ➤ How you select people to hang out with and listen to
- ➤ Who you follow on social media
- ➤ How you make decisions
- ➤ How you vote
- ➤ Your choice of events and conferences
- ➤ How you speak and present yourself

How Contrarian Thinking Can Help Your Business Life

If you're running your own business, we're certain you've looked at your competitors closely, especially the successful ones. You may be tempted to follow their business models to replicate that success. After all, that's what most new business professionals do. They take the safe route and follow trends.

A contrarian doesn't do that, though. They see that the standard model can be improved, and they actively try to improve it. Contrarians modify existing models to create new solutions to existing problems.

When you look at a standard industry from a clean slate, you'll probably see problems that others missed and find ways to fix them. This perspective allows you to tackle customer issues more effectively, maximize profits and do other things that create above-average results.

In short, the contrarian mindset lets you stand out as an innovator in a world of copycats and cookie-cutter businesses. If you go against the grain in the right way, you might even change the world.

We want to give you a few examples of how you can do this and what the results of contrarian thinking as a business professional can be.

If you hop on Amazon and search for a particular product, you're likely to see dozens of listings competing for sales with just minor price differences. These are all crowd followers taking the safe route.

However, you'll often see a brand-new listing for a truly innovative take on that same product, which will be selling well despite having a heftier price tag. Almost certainly, that's a contrarian e-seller. They saw what the crowd was doing, ignored it and found a way to make the product ten times better. As a result, they're getting more sales.

The restaurant business is also a good example of how contrarian thinking can be used. Do you know most new restaurants shut down within their first couple of years of business? The ones that fail all take the same approach: They offer the same food items people can get at more recognizable chains, undersell or oversell the value of their food, and make the same costly decisions that eat up their resources.

The restauranteurs who create beloved community hotspots are the ones that do something new. They don't follow the standard model because it isn't relevant to small establishments. They offer new and exciting foods that customers can't find elsewhere or they work to create a unique dining experience for their customers. They manage their costs in creative ways, too. This is often the case for successful business owners of all kinds. So, try to bring something new to the market.

Using the framework for CT might impact the following:

- ➤ The causes that you embrace
- ➤ How you select problems to solve
- ➤ How you solve issues
- ➤ The way you market your services and solutions
- ➤ How you craft your business narrative
- ➤ How you deal with clients or customers
- ➤ The way you handle competition
- ➤ How you set your products or services apart

> ➢ How you treat employees

> ➢ How you spend your revenue

How Contrarian Thinking Can Help Your Professional Life

Bosses want employees who can make a difference. A bunch of people doing the same thing is useful for getting through day-to-day business, but it's the freethinkers who create positive change within a company.

You can use contrarian thinking to notice issues in a business model and create solutions no one has ever considered. In turn, those solutions can bring new opportunities into your professional life.

You can also use contrarian thinking to show your boss that you're willing to try things your peers aren't or that you can successfully lead a team through new concepts that produce better results.

Following CT principles and using the framework might influence the following:

> ➢ Your career choice

> ➢ Your job searches

> ➢ What you do on the job

> ➢ How you develop your expertise

> ➢ The type of connections you build

> ➢ Your reading choices

> ➤ The types of conferences and training you select to attend

> ➤ How you behave on a team

> ➤ How other people view you

> ➤ Your thoughts on common work or market issues and challenges

> ➤ How you make decisions

> ➤ Your choice of mentors and coaches

> ➤ The types of certifications you obtain

In short, it can change not only the way you work but the way your whole workplace does business.

Contrarian thinking is always useful.

As we demonstrated, contrarian thinking isn't just relevant to hot stock picks or cutting-edge inventions. It can affect every aspect of your life, and you can use it to stand out from the crowd in a lot of constructive ways.

However, we recommend using contrarian thinking in a targeted, purposeful way. Don't just play devil's advocate for the sake of it. Acknowledge a problem, remove any preconceived notions you may have and find a solution on your own. That's how contrarianism makes you stand out.

Resources on Contrarian Thinking

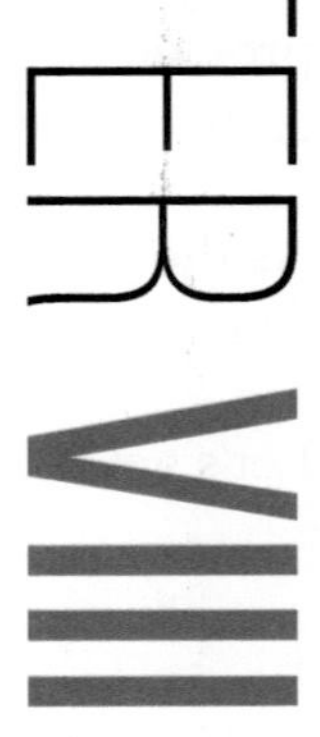

I think what's always important is not to be contrarian for its own sake but to really get at the truth.

— PETER THIEL

We've covered a lot of information on contrarian thinking but absorbing as much information from as many different sources as possible is key to the learning process. To truly develop your contrarian thinking abilities, we know you must constantly expand your knowledge of the subject.

CBL coaching team is all about lifting people to be their best selves. To help you on your journey to developing a contrarian mindset that you can use to excel in the business world and life, we've listed our top books and websites on contrarian thinking here to help you develop faster and more efficiently.

You can implement these into your nightly reading, break-time learning exercises, or whatever works for your routine. All these resources are highly recommended by our coaching team and will be a great use of your time.

Don't stop here, though! When you've exhausted the resources listed here, check out the other references we provide on our website to continue expanding your mind and embracing a contrarian mindset.

As the great contrarian Steve Jobs said, "Learn continuously. There's always 'one more thing' to learn!"

Let's get started!

BOOKS

The Art of Contrary Thinking by Humphrey B. Neill

This book is from 1954 but despite its age, it has remained one of the go-to sources for developing professionals who want to experience the benefits of contrarianism.

The *Art of Contrary Thinking* covers Neill's expert insight into how contrarian thinking has driven the most notable parts of human history.

Moreover, it also explains how influential mass opinions exaggerate issues in the investment field. This helps modern investors understand the purchasing and selling decisions of men like Warren Buffett and other exceptional investors.

Liberating the Mind: Overcoming Sociocentric Thought and Egocentric Tendencies by Dr. Linda Elder

In this book, Dr. Linda Elder, an educational psychologist, discusses how our progress is hindered by our tendency to be biased by not only our own beliefs, but by society's beliefs as well.

From her background in psychology, Elder analyses how people learn, think and act. With her insightful guide, you can learn to liberate yourself from egocentric and sociocentric thinking patterns. Learn to think critically about your biases and free yourself from recycled and repetitive thoughts.

Designing the Mind: The Principles of Psychitecture by Ryan A. Bush

This book pulls from the teachings of great minds throughout history—Marcus Aurelius, Lao Tzu, Friedrich Nietzsche and Abraham Maslow.

Bush combines religion, philosophy, psychology and cognitive therapy to help you with habits, emotions and thoughts you would like to transform.

Long praised by critics, the book can help you, through introspection, understand your mind and learn how to shape it so you can achieve your dreams and goals.

The Contrarian's Guide to Leadership by Steven B. Sample

Whether you're a leader or aspire to become one, this book is for you. Steven B. Sample is praised as the president of the University of Southern California who transformed the institution into the highly rated one it is today.

In this book, he urges readers to think outside the box and travel off the beaten path to make lasting and impactful changes as leaders.

Jenrette: The Contrarian Manager by Richard Jenrette

Jenrette, co-founder of the investment bank Donaldson, Lufkin & Jenrette (DLJ), discusses his business strategies in this must-have contrarian guide. He gives solid advice to leaders, managers and supervisors of any sector and company.

The book also includes an appendix of DLJ's common stock in the 1960s. Consequently, you don't have to take Jenrette's word for it; the evidence shows that being a contrarian manager actually works.

The Contrarian Effect: Why It Pays (Big) to Take Typical Sales Advice and Do the Opposite by Michael Port and Elizabeth Marshall

Tired, traditional sales models don't work anymore. In this book, Port and Marshall explain why it is challenging to stay afloat using these standard models. What's their advice? Abandon them and do the opposite of what people often advise.

In this book, Port and Marshall delve into the system of building relationships with clients, going contrary to conventional wisdom, and enjoying the benefits of increased sales. After all, times have changed. Businesses must evolve with their customers.

Contrarian Investment Strategies: The Psychological Edge by David Dreman

In this book, Dreman discusses the flaws in most investment strategies from a psychological point of view. According to him, the most popular strategies tend to fail because they do not take human nature and reasoning into account.

Using psychological findings, Dreman introduces his own contrarian investment strategies. These take human thinking and behaviors into account so you can be an intelligent investor.

The Acquirer's Multiple: How the Billionaire Contrarians of Deep Value Beat the Market by Tobias E. Carlisle

This book by Carlisle details how Warren Buffett, Carl Icahn, David Einhorn and Daniel Loeb became prosperous investors and continue to make successful decisions throughout their careers.

Carlisle, who is also a value investor, engages the reader with stories while backing up his claims and advice with data and research. If you're a beginning investor, this book will be a great resource for you. It helps new investors understand investments and make that first step by taking the off-beaten path to financial success.

Letters to a Young Contrarian: Art of Mentoring by Christopher Hitchens

Best-selling author, Christopher Hitchens, explores the ramifications of being contrary in a world that seeks only agreement and harmony.

Hitchens sees disagreement as essential for personal growth, discussion and societal progress. As he makes his case, he challenges prevailing views with wit and an inspiring tone. This is a great book to get a sense of how being a contrarian thinker will change your life.

Think Again: Contrarian Reflections on Life, Culture, Politics, Religion, Law, and Education by Stanley Fish

Fish is considered one of America's most influential thinkers. In this book, his goal is to teach you how to think instead of what to think.

In this collection of essays, Fish analyzes various topics from different perspectives: life, culture, politics, religion, law and education. He then points out the flaws in common approaches to each area.

As a bonus, he also provides autobiographical essays where you learn about his fears, aspirations, and other parts of Fish that are often hidden behind his tough analyses.

Extraordinary Popular Delusions and the Madness of Crowds by Charles Mackay

This 1841 publication by Charles Mackay is an outlier, published decades before most of the other resources listed here. However, it's an important and remarkable look at how people think, which is highly relevant to understanding the value of going against the grain.

Rather than writing a book directly meant to encourage contrarian thinking, Charles Mackay opted to highlight the negative effects of mass opinion in an approach that relies heavily on entertaining anecdotes and humor.

For the modern-day contrarian, Mackay's book functions as a humorous and sometimes sensational example of how important contrarianism truly is.

WEBSITES

These resources were current and up to date as of publication. The web is a constantly shifting landscape, however, so browse carefully.

contrarian-investing.com

This website is dedicated to providing up-to-date guidance, tips and other resources for contrarian investors.

The guidance is useful for budding investors or investors just starting to go against the crowd so they can make real headway in the investment arena.

The site also regularly adds informative guides to developing your contrarian mindset; we couldn't recommend it more strongly to those now starting on their contrarian investment journey.

criticalthinking.org

This website is dedicated to promoting critical thinking and educational reform.

It is rich in resources designed to guide you to think critically about different aspects of your life. It also provides a library of resources, including research done by The Center for Critical Thinking and Moral Critique and the Foundation for Critical Thinking.

You can also check out their regularly updated calendars of events and conferences, accredited online courses and critical thinking assessments.

truecontrarian.com

Steven Jon Kaplan began this blog in 1996 and has been updating it ever since. That's over two decades of invaluable advice from a registered investment advisor with a track record of success.

The site has evolved from a weekly blog and to a daily newsletter with expanded content. Now, he regularly posts his entertaining and helpful views on global financial markets.

contrarianedge.com

Vitaliy Katsenelson, who started ContrarianEdge, is an investor, writer and educator. On his site, he shares his opinions and advice on investing, music and life.

You can sign up to receive his articles, which are not available anywhere else. You can also buy his books that explore contrarian thinking on investing, sideways markets and the electric vehicle revolution.

alanweiss.com/blog

This site is all about contrarian consulting.

Alan Weiss is a consultant, speaker and author. He has advised major companies such as Mercedes-Benz, The New York Times and Toyota. On his blog, you can find snippets of his humorous reflections and points of view on various topics, from investing to the hospitality industry.

contrarianliving.blog

Change how you think about money and life with Niraj Dugar's insightful blog.

Contrarian Living aims to help you achieve financial freedom and become more aware of opportunities in the financial world. It encourages you to think about your relationship with money differently, whether it is your spending habits, returns or holding stocks.

thequintessentialmind.com

The Quintessential Mind is another site that can aid you in your journey to becoming a contrarian as it offers several resources on some of the more philosophical aspects of personal and financial growth.

Its purpose is to help people become well-rounded, independent and purposeful thinkers who excel in life. So, it should be one of your top choices for nightly reading.

contrarianthinking.co

This is an online tool dedicated to helping contrarian professionals increase their cash flow. You'll find guidance blogs, weekly newsletters, tools for preparing your investments, and plenty of cash flow ideas that cater to the contrarian mindset.

boardofinnovation.com

Board of Innovation prides itself on helping business professionals reach their true potential. They've made multiple PDF tools available to help you track your development or identify where you're going wrong. They also offer a multitude of original content on contrarianism and other useful mindsets.

bankrate.com

If you're a contrarian in the business field, money means a lot to you. Bankrate not only has information on how you can use contrarian thinking to further your financial life, but it offers the banking tools you'll need to facilitate any changes you may need to make.

The site's main focus is on setting you up for a successful retirement through good financial decisions in the present.

constantrenewal.com

Constant Renewal is a must-see resource that dives into the philosophical aspects of contrarianism. The site often calls out fake contrarians, pushes you to embody the contrarian mindset positively, and provides plenty of insight into the ironic popularity of contrarianism.

The priceless insight offered here can help you develop your mind and life in more ways than one.

We appreciate all of our readers, and we hope that, from these pages, you've come to learn a lot about contrarian thinking and developing your life in general.

However, we know that no single source will ever cover every detail of such a complex topic. That's why we've curated and presented a range of high-quality external resources and references. As you explore the content we suggest, remember to branch out; find new resources on your own and, of course, always think for yourself as a true contrarian.

Start reading today.

At Coaching for Better Learning (CBL), we want to provide our readers with quick, reliable access to as many useful educational tools and resources as possible. The resource lists we provide will give you a rich range of material to browse during your developmental journey. They are a good starting point. Some are from great contrarian minds of the past, and some are modern, investment-based resources that help people of all experience levels.

Working these resources into your regular reading routine will help you understand contrarianism a bit more, and we guarantee it'll help expand your mind and push your progression forward.

CONCLUSION

> *The most contrarian thing of all is not to oppose the crowd but to think for yourself.*
> - **PETER THIEL**

In this book, we've demonstrated how you can use contrarian thinking to take your career or business to the next level. As you know, the job market is highly competitive. Therefore, doing what everybody does and thinking the way they do is very likely to make you stagnant or stuck in competition with others. If you want to enjoy different results, you need to act and think differently from the people around you.

This book also uses concrete examples to show you that thinking for yourself or not letting people do your thinking for you is the best way to be a trailblazer and a pathfinder in your field or job. However, we also argue that one should use contrarian thinking wisely. It should be adapted to your situation and culture.

Moreover, the framework and resources we've provided will serve you well in exploring the impact of contrarian thinking and how you can apply it to your own life. We hope you take advantage of what we've presented here to further your understanding of why thinking differently is valuable. And, of course, don't just take our word for it and follow everything we say. Ask questions, read the resources critically, and come to your own conclusions. After all, that's the whole point of contrarian thinking—finding a mindset that works for you.

We hope these pages help you understand and see the value of using contrarian thinking. We did our part. Now it's your turn.

As you embark on your contrarian thinking journey, please do us one small favor: gift this book to someone who also wants to think differently from the crowd. Share the power of thinking for yourself and help someone else find the means and the courage to go against the flow.

Thank you, and good luck!

REFERENCES

A&E Networks Television. (2019, October 24). *Mark Zuckerberg*. Biography.com. Retrieved December 31, 2021, from https://www.biography.com/business-figure/mark-zuckerberg

Bankrate. (n.d.). Retrieved December 31, 2021, from https://www.bankrate.com/

Blog. Contrarian Living. (n.d.). Retrieved December 31, 2021, from https://contrarianliving.blog/blog/

Bush, R. A. (2021). *Designing the mind: The principles of psychitecture*. Designing the Mind.

Carlisle, T. E. (2017). *The acquirer's multiple: How the billionaire contrarians of deep value beat the market*. Ballymore Publishing.

Constant renewal. Constant Renewal. (2021, May 7). Retrieved December 31, 2021, from https://constantrenewal.com/

Contrarian consulting. Alan Weiss, PhD. (2021, December 31). Retrieved December 31, 2021, from https://alanweiss.com/blog/

Contrarian investing: Financial guides, investment insights and market analysis. Contrarian Investing. (n.d.). Retrieved December 31, 2021, from https://www.contrarian-investing.com/

Contrarian thinking. Contrarian Thinking. (2021, December 20). Retrieved December 31, 2021, from https://contrarianthinking.co/

Dreman, D. (2012). *Contrarian Investment Strategies: The psychological edge.* Free Press.

Elder, L. (2019). *Liberating the mind: Overcoming sociocentric thought and egocentric tendencies.* Rowman & Littlefield Publishing Group.

Fish, S. (2015). *Think again: Contrarian reflections on life, culture, politics, religion, law, and education.* Princeton University Press.

Fred Carl, Jr. Viking Range, LLC. (n.d.). Retrieved December 31, 2021, from https://www.vikingrange.com/consumer/category/more-viking/the-viking-story/fred-carl--jr-

Hitchens, C. (2001). *Letters to a young contrarian.* Basic Books.

Iliopoulos, A. The Quintessential Mind. (n.d.). Retrieved December 31, 2021, from https://thequintessentialmind.com/

Jenrette, R. H. (1997). *Jenrette, the contrarian manager.* McGraw-Hill.

Katsenelson, V. (2021, December 20). Contrarian Edge. Retrieved December 31, 2021, from https://contrarianedge.com/

Mackay, C. (1841). *Extraordinary popular delusions and the madness of crowds.* Richard Bentley.

Mey, N. D. (2021, August 24). *Business Design & Innovation Strategy Firm.* Board of Innovation. Retrieved December 31, 2021, from https://www.boardofinnovation.com/

Neill, Humphrey B. (1954). *The art of contrary thinking.* Caxton Press.

Port, M., & Marshall, E. (2008). *The contrarian effect why it pays (big) to take typical sales advice and do the opposite.* Wiley.

Sample, S. B. (2003). *The Contrarian's Guide to Leadership.* Jossey-Bass.

The Foundation for Critical Thinking. (n.d.). Retrieved December 31, 2021, from https://www.criticalthinking.org/

True contrarian by Steven Jon Kaplan. True Contrarian by Steven Jon Kaplan. (n.d.). Retrieved December 31, 2021, from http://truecontrarian.com/

INDEX

ABOUT THE AUTHOR

Coach Teddy Edouard is a lifelong learner, public speaker, writer, blogger and vlogger. He is the Systems and Learning Coach at Coaching for Better Learning LLC, where he helps people and institutions build systems that lead to lasting improvement, growth and success.

Teddy also teaches professionals how to protect their careers and use artificial intelligence (AI) as a career improvement ally. You can say "hello" to him on Twitter (TeddyISD) and LinkedIn.

If you are looking for a contrarian keynote speaker, a systems thinker and builder, or a learning expert for your face-to-face or virtual events and podcasts, contact Teddy at **teamcbl@coachingforbetterlearning.com** or Visit **https://coachingforbetterlearning.com/speaking-engagement/**.

ALSO BY TEDDY EDOUARD

Creating Winning Career Systems

ABOUT

CBL helps build Continuous Improvement (CI) systems that lead to stress-free improvement, growth and sustainable success.

We offer reliable client-centered systems building coaching services to help you face your challenges with more confidence and less anxiety. Visit us at coachingforbetterlearning.com

Check our blog out:
https://coachingforbetterlearning.com/blog.

Printed by Libri Plureos GmbH in Hamburg,
Germany